Save Our Sand Dunes

W0017296

© 2024 by the North Carolina Office of Archives and History
All rights reserved.

978-0-8652-6505-9

D. Reid Wilson
Secretary, North Carolina Department of Natural and Cultural Resources

Dr. Darin J. Waters
Deputy Secretary, Office of Archives and History

Ramona Bartos
Director, Division of Historical Resources

Ansley Herring Wegner
Research Supervisor

Sheilah Barrett Carroll
Book Designer

NORTH CAROLINA HISTORICAL COMMISSION

David Ruffin (2023)
CHAIR

Dr. Mary Lynn Bryan (2023)	Barbara Groome (2025)
The Honorable Newell Clark (2027)	Dr. Valerie Ann Johnson (2027)
Shana Bushyhead Condill (2025)	Susan Phillips (2025)
Dr. David Dennard (2027)	W. Noah Reynolds (2023)
Samuel B. Dixon (2025)	Barbara B. Snowden (2023)

EMERITI: Millie M. Barbee, Narvel J. Crawford, Alan D. Watson

Distributed by the University of North Carolina Press.

Heartfelt thanks to the Baum family for sharing family photos on pages 18 and 22.

Special thanks to Mat Waehner, photographer with the North Carolina Office of Archives and History,
for photographing the cover and interior illustrations in the book.

Special thanks to the North Carolina Outer Banks History Center for the photo of Carolista Baum on page 10.

Special thanks to the North Carolina State Parks and Recreation for sharing a photo on page 19, and maps that appear on pages 24 and 25.

COVER ILLUSTRATION: Larry McCarter
INTERIOR ILLUSTRATIONS: Larry McCarter's illustrations are on pages i, iii, iv, v, vi, 1, 2, 3, 8, 9, 16, 20, 21 and 26. Anne Marshall Runyon's illustrations are on pages 4, 5, 6, and 7. iStock photos on pages 11 and 12.

"We have a heritage unlike any other country . . .
I think we owe the preservation of nature [Jockey's Ridge]
and other good things about our country to the future."

Carolista

This book is dedicated to all of the children, and children at heart, who love a place enough to know when not to give up on it. We thank our mom for leading our way with persistence and creativity; and for never taking "no" for an answer. Her legacy lives on in everyone who visits Jockey's Ridge State Park.

ANN-CABELL, INGLIS, AND GIBBS BAUM

On the edge of the Atlantic, there is a stretch of sand called the Outer Banks. They are barrier islands, which can be found all along the North Carolina coast. But one of them has something special—a sand dune that is taller, wider, and bigger than all the rest. Its name is Jockey's Ridge. Today, it is the most visited State Park in North Carolina. But years ago, this striking natural wonder was nearly destroyed, until three children used their voices to help save it.

History and Unique Ecology of Jockey's Ridge

Jockey's Ridge is the tallest sand dune system in the Eastern United States. It is often called a "living" dune because it is always changing and shifting. An entire miniature golf course is buried underneath it! The tip of a castle that was part of the course is sometimes visible today, poking up out of the sand.

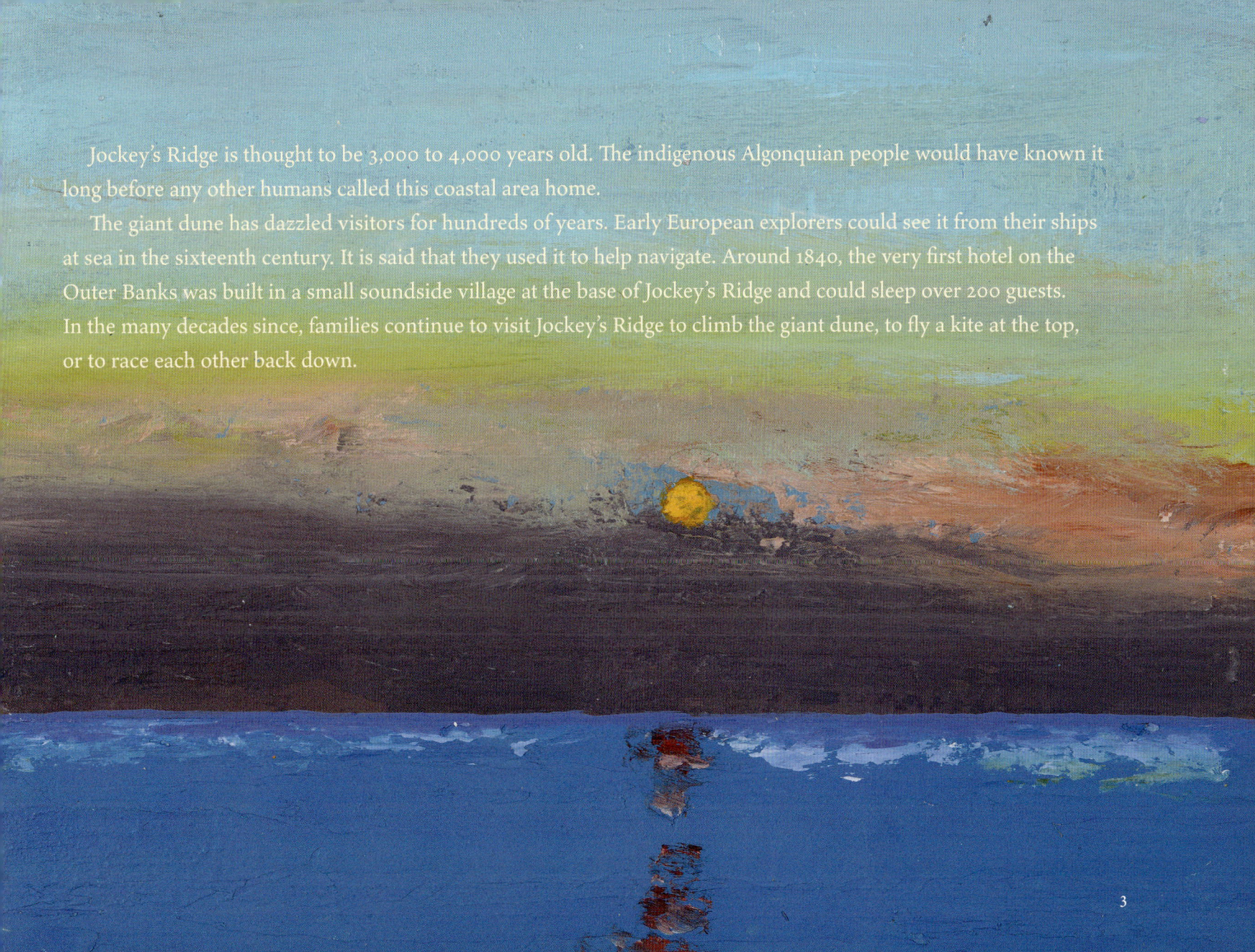

Jockey's Ridge is thought to be 3,000 to 4,000 years old. The indigenous Algonquian people would have known it long before any other humans called this coastal area home.

The giant dune has dazzled visitors for hundreds of years. Early European explorers could see it from their ships at sea in the sixteenth century. It is said that they used it to help navigate. Around 1840, the very first hotel on the Outer Banks was built in a small soundside village at the base of Jockey's Ridge and could sleep over 200 guests. In the many decades since, families continue to visit Jockey's Ridge to climb the giant dune, to fly a kite at the top, or to race each other back down.

The dune is made up of three sandy peaks, with no vegetation atop them. But grasses like American Beach Grass and trees like pine, sweet gum, and wax myrtle grow at its base. The tall dune protects the plant life from the wind and the salt spray coming off the ocean. Foxes, raccoons, and deer make their homes in these maritime thickets as well. It is a rare and delicate ecosystem.

The Roanoke Sound on the back side of the dune is an estuary where freshwater and saltwater mix. Marsh grasses like cattails and black needlerush create habitats for crabs, fish, and coastal birds.

6

There are over **400** different bird species that have been identified at the the Outer Banks. The birds on this page are more frequently seen at Jockey's Ridge State Park. Have you seen any of these birds at Jockey's Ridge or at other areas of the Outer Banks?

Osprey

Black Skimmer

Pelican

Piping Plover

Sanderlings

A Strange Sound

One day in 1973, three siblings set out from their family's cottage on the oceanfront in Nags Head. They headed for Jockey's Ridge, as they did most days of their sunkissed summers on the Outer Banks. Once they were helped to safely cross the road, they were free to climb the dune and roam among its many wonders. They explored its high ridges and low freshwater pools, thickets of oak, and grassy soundside beaches. They climbed the face of the giant dune up to its tallest point and then raced each other back down, breathless and laughing in a sandy heap at the bottom. When the sun set behind the towering dune at day's end, the sky melted into molten orange, pink, and purple.

Jockey's Ridge was a personal playground for Ann-Cabell, her sister Inglis, and their brother Gibbs. It was a magical place where they could hear squawking gulls, the whistling wind, and the gentle lapping of waves. But on this day, they heard something odd and out of place. They followed the low, rumbling sound across the sands until they found a bulldozer, ready to dig into the base of the dune.

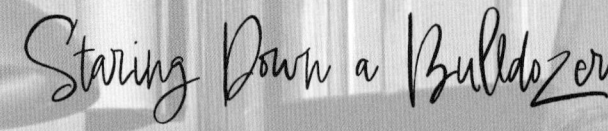

Staring Down a Bulldozer

This time, after racing down the dune at Jockey's Ridge, the kids kept running. Back on the oceanside, their mother was working in her jewelry store. She skillfully crafted one-of-a-kind pieces with stones and gems adorned in silver and gold. Her name was Carolista, and she was known for making beautiful jewelry. But she was also known for getting things done.

Ann-Cabell, Inglis, and Gibbs came bursting in with news of the heavy machinery they encountered on the ridge. Carolista stood up from her work bench. She was alarmed, but also determined. She marched over to Jockey's Ridge with her three children trailing behind. She was upset by the idea of such an historic and important natural landmark being disturbed or developed, the same as her kids.

When they reached the dune, they kicked off their shoes and started up the steepest part of the hill. Reaching the top, they could see the bulldozer and a few other vehicles on the other side. Some had begun to push loads of sand into trucks that were hauling it off. Carolista walked right up to the bulldozer. She stood in front of it and motioned for it to stop.

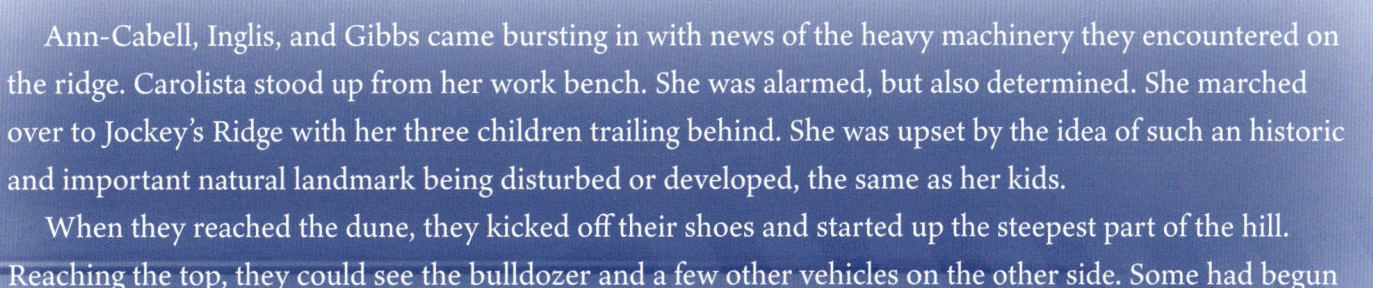

The bulldozer operator climbed down off the machine. He told her that his company was flattening this section of the dune to build condominiums. The children thought this was an odd idea, since Carolista had told them how some of the houses built here long ago had been covered up and buried by the shifting sands. They wondered what would happen to all of the animals that lived there. They worried about their playground and all the folks who liked to visit this special place.

Then they watched their mother plant her feet in the sand in front of the bulldozer and refuse to move. She stood for the land, for the animals, for her children, and all the people. Unable to keep working, the men abandoned their machines and left for the day. Carolista knew it was time to figure out her next move. She was determined to save Jockey's Ridge, and her kids were going to help her.

PETITION TO SAVE JOCKEY'S RIDGE

Save Our Sand Dunes

We, the undersigned, respectfully petition the State of North Carolina to purchase Jockey's Ridge and its surrounding area to preserve and protect this natural wonder that affords so much enjoyment to all citizens of the land.

Jockey's Ridge, the highest sand dune on the east coast of the United States of America, is one of North Carolina's premier scenic attractions. With the Wright Brother's Monument, the Cape Hatteras Lighthouse, and the Lost Colony, Jockey's Ridge is a major tourist attraction; it is also a

Wasting no time, Carolista penned a petition to the state of North Carolina called "Save Our Sand Dunes." With the help of her family, it got 25,000 signatures in the first week. This was remarkable since there were only around 8,000 people living in the area at that time. It showed just how many people had a special place in their hearts for the natural beauty of the Outer Banks, even those who lived far from it.

Next, the unstoppable Carolista formed a group called The People to Preserve Jockey's Ridge. She told everyone she could about her plans to save the giant dune, and she got Ann-Cabell, Inglis, and Gibbs to help. Their mother believed that no one was too small to make a difference, and so they believed it too. They helped her come up with creative ideas to raise money so that their group could purchase as much of the land as they could, with the dream of it one day becoming a state park.

A petition signed by local citizens and tourists to save Jockey's Ridge from destruction, 1973.

bright pink hut!

Durham Morning Herald

Crusade Mounted To Save Dune
State Urged To Buy Jockey Ridge For State Park

Sandy Landmark At Nags Head
Ecological Campaign Waged To Insure Dune Keeps Its...

SOS: SAVE OUR SAND DUNES!
JOCKEY'S RIDGE, NAGS HEAD, N.C.
DESIGNED & PRODUCED BY ART GUILD INC. RICHMOND, VA.

The Charlotte Observer

C&D Board Action
Jockey Ridge Park Backed

Kids all over the Outer Banks collected spare change in cardboard canisters that said "SOS! Save Our Sand Dunes." The People to Preserve Jockey's Ridge sold bumper stickers, T-shirts, notepads, kites, and more, all printed with the same message. The three Baum children were excited to have their very own headquarters where they could help with the cause. Carolista had a bright pink wooden hut moved near the dune where Ann-Cabell, Inglis, and Gibbs collected donations.

14

One of the handmade posters created for the Save Sand Dune 1973 campaign. A set of collages created to promote the preservation of Jockey's Ridge. Includes articles from the *Durham Morning Herald* and the *Charlotte Observer*.

They were also put in charge of dialing and redialing phone numbers on the old rotary phone while their mother worked. When the person on the other end of the line picked up, they would pass the phone to Carolista so she could work her magic. She was charming and kind, but persistent. She spoke with members of local government, state officials, and important people in the community who could help with the cause. She drove to the governor's office in Raleigh every day for three weeks straight, demanding to see the governor or any legislator that would listen. She wanted to know what she had to do to save Jockey's Ridge.

Jim Hunt, lieutenant governor at the time, was receptive to her idea. Years later he remarked, "I remember who 'hounded me' the most about our natural resources—it was Carolista Baum. I have never seen anybody who worked harder on something, who was absolutely committed, and she wouldn't take 'no' for an answer."

And it worked! Carolista's activism convinced the governor's office that the dune was worth saving and they were willing to use state resources to help make it happen.

JAMES B. HUNT, JR.
GOVERNOR OF NORTH CAROLINA
1977-1985   1993-2001

As North Carolina's longest serving Governor, I remember who "hounded me" the most about our natural resources. It was Carolista Baum. She had a passion to save Jockey's Ridge. She would get up early, drive to Raleigh, and demand that the Governor's Office get her in to see me and tell me "what I must do to save Jockey's Ridge." I agreed with her and I pitched in to help save it.

Thank goodness we have Jockey's Ridge and that Carolista "made us save it."

Sincerely,

James B. Hunt, Jr.
Governor of North Carolina
1977-1985, 1993-2001

CAMPUS BOX 7406 · RALEIGH, NC 27695-7406

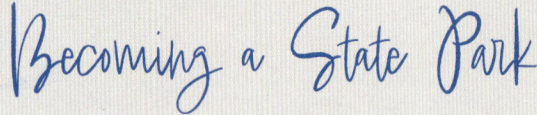

Becoming a State Park

After studying the area, North Carolina's Parks and Recreation Division determined that the idea to turn Jockey's Ridge into a state park would work. Land inside of state parks is protected from building and development. State parks are cared for by park rangers and open to everyone who wants to enjoy the beautiful nature and special landmarks across North Carolina.

The following year, in 1974, Jockey's Ridge was declared a Natural National Landmark. This was a victory, but it didn't mean that the land was protected just yet. There was one problem: the land belonged to other people. It would need to be purchased from several local Nags Head families who owned it. The good news was that the owners agreed that Jockey's Ridge should be preserved and protected as well.

In 1975, the state of North Carolina bought 152 acres of land to create Jockey's Ridge State Park. The Nature Conservancy bought another large section of the land, which included Nags Head Woods, as well. The rest of the land for the park was purchased by the People to Preserve Jockey's Ridge. They threw a big party called the Jockey's Ridge Jamboree right on top of the dune. They celebrated handing the land over to the state so that no bulldozer could ever threaten it again.

All of the donations that the Baum children collected in the bright pink hut, all of the loose change collected by their friends, all of the t-shirts, bumper stickers, phone calls and visits to the governor's office had paid off. Thanks to three kids who deeply loved a sand dune and their mother, Carolista, Jockey's Ridge was saved.

Inglis, Ann-Cabell, and Gibbs Baum at Jockeys Ridge, 1974 (*left to right*).

Jockey's Ridge Today

Today, Jockey's Ridge is the most visited state park in North Carolina, with over one million visitors a year! In the 1990s, a group called the Friends of Jockey's Ridge was formed. They followed in Carolista's footsteps, raising money to build a visitor's center, a boardwalk, and nature trails in the park. The plants, fish, birds, and animals that make their homes in the ecosystems within the park are safe and protected. Visitors enjoy ranger programs, activities for kids, nature hikes, hang gliding, kite flying, and breathtaking sunsets. And of course, racing each other down the dune. The road leading into the park is called Carolista Drive.

Remembering Carolista

In 2023, a group gathered on the side of Carolista Drive at the entrance to the park. Ann-Cabell, Inglis, and Gibbs were there with their families. They were all grown up. They loved being together on Jockey's Ridge again, just as they were when they were kids. The sun that day shone as brightly as their mother's smile. They were all gathered to remember and celebrate Carolista by dedicating a highway historical marker in honor of her hard work. The crowd watched as the marker was unveiled. When the black cloth was pulled away, everyone clapped and cheered. The marker reads:

B 78
CAROLISTA BAUM
1940-1991
Environmental activist. Stopped destruction of Jockey's Ridge sand dune in 1973. Fundraised and lobbied to preserve as a N.C. State Park, 1975.

NORTH CAROLINA OFFICE OF ARCHIVES AND HISTORY   2022

The next time you climb Jockey's Ridge, the tallest sand dune in the east, remember Carolista. Remember how her three children were the spark that started the story of a beloved state park. When you use *your voice* to stand up for what matters, what might *you* spark?

My Jockey's Ridge Trip Scrapbook Page!

Where is Jockey's Ridge in North Carolina?

You were here!

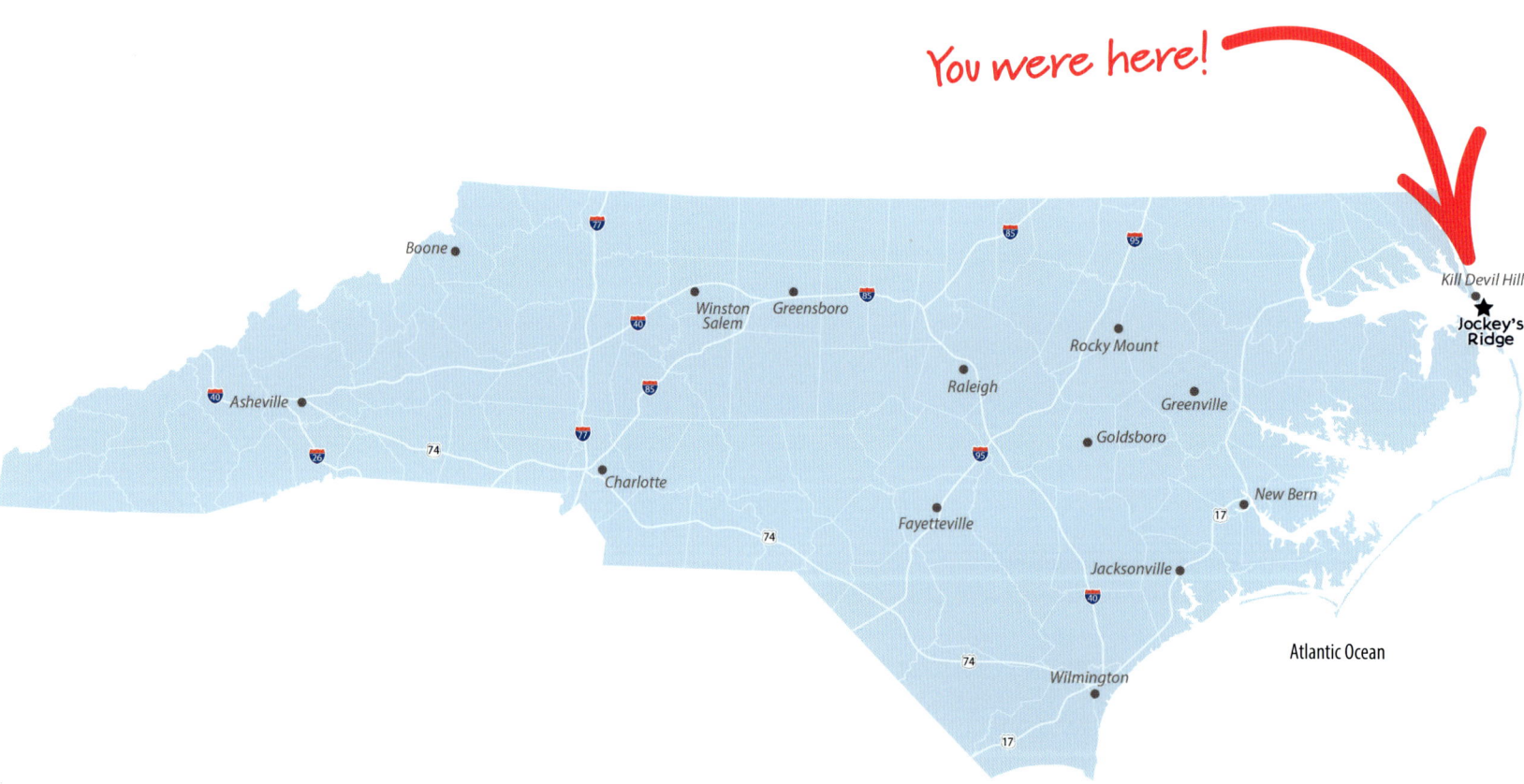

Boone

Winston Salem

Greensboro

Asheville

Rocky Mount

Raleigh

Greenville

Charlotte

Goldsboro

Fayetteville

New Bern

Jacksonville

Atlantic Ocean

Wilmington

Kill Devil Hills

Jockey's Ridge

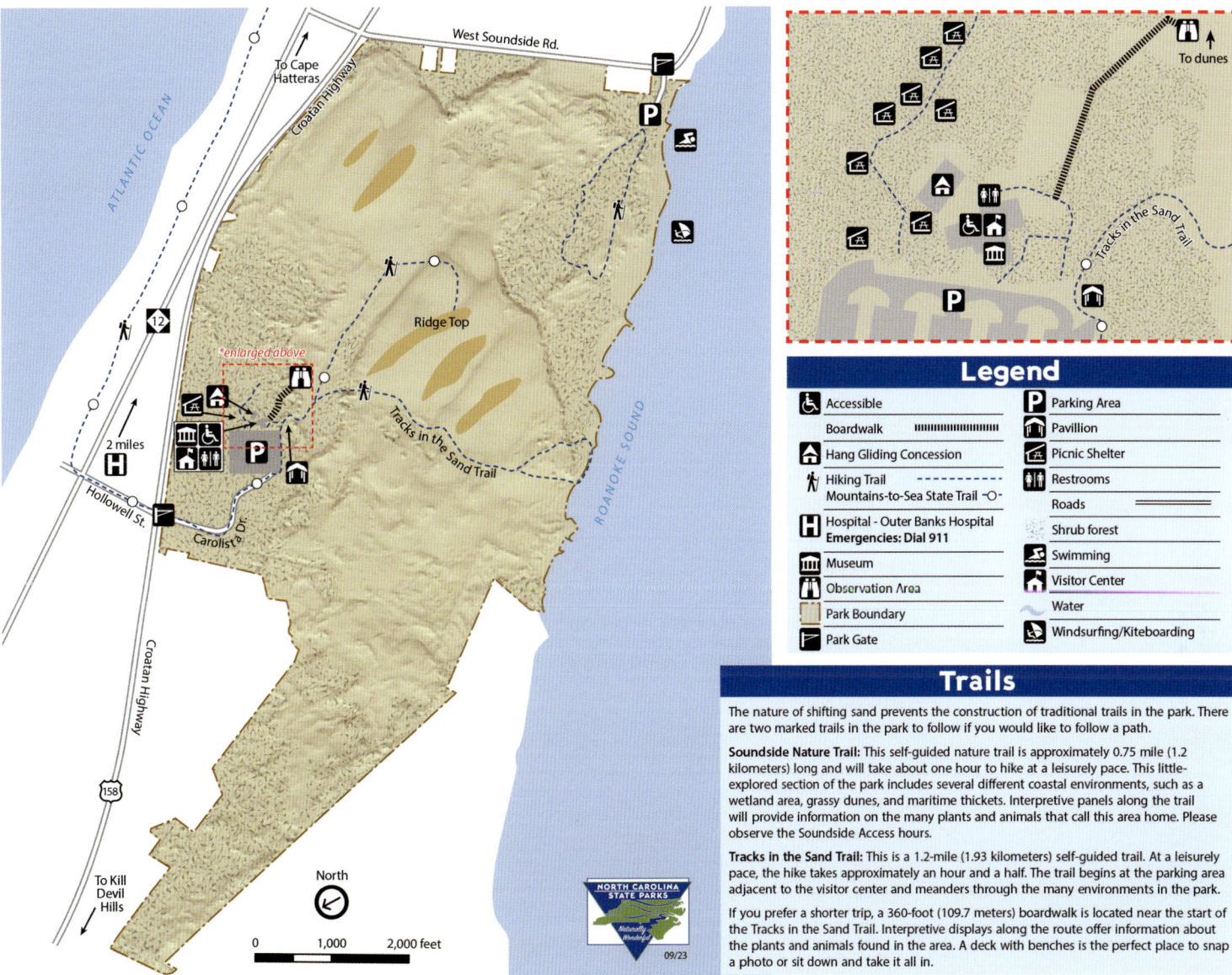

West Soundside Rd.

To Cape Hatteras

Croatan Highway

ATLANTIC OCEAN

To dunes

enlarged above

Ridge Top

Tracks in the Sand Trail

2 miles

Hollowell St.

Carolista Dr.

Croatan Highway

158

To Kill Devil Hills

ROANOKE SOUND

Tracks in the Sand Trail

Legend

♿	Accessible	P	Parking Area
	Boardwalk		Pavillion
🏠	Hang Gliding Concession		Picnic Shelter
🚶	Hiking Trail Mountains-to-Sea State Trail	🚻	Restrooms
H	Hospital - Outer Banks Hospital **Emergencies: Dial 911**		Roads
🏛	Museum		Shrub forest
	Observation Area		Swimming
	Park Boundary		Visitor Center
⚑	Park Gate	~	Water
			Windsurfing/Kiteboarding

North

0   1,000   2,000 feet

NORTH CAROLINA STATE PARKS
Naturally Wonderful
09/23

Trails

The nature of shifting sand prevents the construction of traditional trails in the park. There are two marked trails in the park to follow if you would like to follow a path.

Soundside Nature Trail: This self-guided nature trail is approximately 0.75 mile (1.2 kilometers) long and will take about one hour to hike at a leisurely pace. This little-explored section of the park includes several different coastal environments, such as a wetland area, grassy dunes, and maritime thickets. Interpretive panels along the trail will provide information on the many plants and animals that call this area home. Please observe the Soundside Access hours.

Tracks in the Sand Trail: This is a 1.2-mile (1.93 kilometers) self-guided trail. At a leisurely pace, the hike takes approximately an hour and a half. The trail begins at the parking area adjacent to the visitor center and meanders through the many environments in the park.

If you prefer a shorter trip, a 360-foot (109.7 meters) boardwalk is located near the start of the Tracks in the Sand Trail. Interpretive displays along the route offer information about the plants and animals found in the area. A deck with benches is the perfect place to snap a photo or sit down and take it all in.

About the Authors

HANNAH BUNN WEST grew up on the Outer Banks and is passionate about sharing its history, advocating for its people, and protecting its natural wonders. She is a freelance writer, former teacher, and the author of *Remarkable Women of the Outer Banks*. She lives in Kill Devil Hills with her husband and two children.

ANN-CABELL BAUM grew up in Nags Head across from Jockey's Ridge. She is the oldest daughter of Carolista Fletcher Baum, artist, jeweler, preservationist, and great granddaughter of Inglis Fletcher, a noted historian and author instrumental in the development of the Elizabethan Gardens in Manteo. Ann-Cabell is a successful business woman in Raleigh, N.C., and vice chairwoman of the Friends of Jockey's Ridge State Park.